THE PRESS OF THE TERRITORIAN
PRESENTS
Number **7** of a Series
 Of Western Americana

Adolphe Francis Alphonse
BANDELIER

BY

JACK SCHAEFER

ADOLPHE FRANCIS ALPHONSE BANDELIER
August 6, 1840----March 19, 1914

He was born far away and he died far away and he was forty years old before he went west and when he went he did so as a superior civilized being looking down a studious nose at barbarians and stone-age people and he stayed only the better part of eleven years. But he belongs to the west, to the southwest. Without particularly intending to, without doing anything more than pursuing his studies with single-minded zeal, he made himself as much a part of it as the ancient ruins he measured and the mountains and deserts he trod. Whatever of the energy and spirit that were Adolphe Bandelier remains anywhere, it remains in the American southwest.

He was born in August of 1840 in Berne, Switzerland, of a family long distinguished in the town. His father was a well educated intelligent man, an amateur scientist, an officer in the Swiss army, criminal judge for the Berne district. His mother had been briefly married before, when quite young, to another Swiss officer and had spent time with him in St. Petersburg where she had known the gaiety of court life. It was probably that sojourn in Russia which prompted the persistent later legend that she was of Russian, even of noble Russian birth.

Adolphe was their one child. As soon as he could talk and toddle about the family castle in Berne, both parents began tutoring him. By the time he was six he was already a linguist, fluent in French and German and becoming acquainted with Italian and English.

In 1847 political troubles brought an abrupt change. There is an old story that on one occasion a cannon was trained on the castle and the family forced to flee. As so often in those days, political turmoil in Europe was pointing able educated independent people towards the New World. The father and a friend went to Brazil searching for a suitable place for new homes. Disgusted at conditions there, they returned to Switzerland. A little later the father tried again,

3

came to the United States, looked over the possibilities along the then frontier of settlement, and bought a tract of land near the new little town of Highland in Illinois. Satisfied this time, he sent for the rest of the family.

Young Adolphe may have attended school in Highland. Certainly not for long. He was already or at least soon well beyond what schooling could yet be found there. But in his mother, until her death when he was in his early teens, he had a good teacher. And in his father he had an excellent one. The family spoke the various languages together to keep in practice. They read aloud together in the evenings. They had a telescope with which they studied the heavens. They were not far from St. Louis, emerging cultural center of the midwest, and competent men in many fields from there and points eastward visited the Bandelier home and long talks and arguments were frequent. Adolphe was acquiring a breadth of knowledge remarkable not only for his youth but for his time and place in America. Already the spirit of scientific inquiry was taking hold of him. In 1855, all of fifteen, he returned to Switzerland to study at the University of Berne.

He spent several years at the university, studying under and meeting many scientists, among them Alexander von Humboldt, the great German naturalist, who made a strong impression on him. By the late 1850's he was back at Highland. In 1860, now all of twenty, he married Josephine Huegy, four years older than himself and of appropriate Swiss parentage.

For the next twenty years he tried to be a practical businessman. Was a businessman. His father was an important man in the Highland area, interested in many enterprises. Adolphe worked in the bank established by his father and several partners. He managed the family foundry and the family coal-mine. He worked long and hard. But he was a misfit in business. He disliked it. He loathed it. He had to drive himself to it. To him it was plain drudgery with no mental stimulus. His true interest was in the studies he was pursuing in the evenings and on Sundays and during every spare moment.

He had come under the influence of Lewis Henry Morgan, the "father of American ethnology".

Morgan was a retired eastern attorney (his home was in Rochester, New York) who was busy refuting the claim of classical archaeologists that no significant discoveries could be achieved in the Americas by making the first truly scientific investigations of American Indians.

He had already completed his work on the government and social organization of the Iroquois and was developing his theory (he had many of them) that the Aztecs of Mexico were of Pueblo stock which had drifted southward out of New Mexico. He had visited in the Bandelier home. Adolphe was in frequent correspondence with him. Adolphe, with the profound reverence of a disciple for a master, was busy trying to buttress Morgan's theories with scholarly data. He was making himself a well-read student in ethnology and archaeology and history, particularly the history of Latin America as recorded by the Spanish conquistadores. Sometime along the way, a simple accomplishment for him, he had become a thorough scholar in Spanish. He was doing what Morgan was not equipped to do, digging into the original sources in the original language.

In the long perspective, his relationship with Morgan was both a liability and an asset. It was a liability in that it pushed him into fixed convictions that would mar his own later work. Morgan was a man of unshakable opinions. He believed, for example, that basically there were only two forms of government, one based on persons, on personal relations, the other on territory and property, and that inevitably any people anywhere progressed in time from the one to the other. He believed absolutely that all Amerindians, all Indians of the American continents, had been at the time of Columbus and still were only in the first phase---and also that all Amerindian tribes would be found to have the same basic social organization as the Iroquois. Adolphe, in this formative stage of his own thinking, sometimes had a tough time swallowing his master's strictures in their entirety. Whenever his own judgment and interpretation of apparent facts seemed to dispute the master, he pulled back and wrote of his doubts and was persuaded anew. By sheer persistence and mental discipline over many years he forced himself into virtually complete acceptance of Morgan's theories. The rest of his life he would often be struggling to compel stubborn facts to conform to those theories.

The relationship was an asset, however, far outweighing the handicap, in that it gave point and purpose to the spare-time studies that were becoming ever more his real existence. It kept his enthusiasm strong and made him a personal friend of the last years of the currently most important pioneer in the whole field of Amerindian studies. Through Morgan he made the acquaintance, personally and by letters, of many others working in the same field and received rare books and papers he would otherwise have had considerable difficulty trying to obtain. It was Morgan who at last gave him the push into his true career.

He was killing himself by inches, this tough-minded and tough-sinewed but smallish and bookish Adolphe Francis Alphonse Bandelier--trying to be a businessman and a scholar at the same time: Working hard at the one during the days, working equally hard at the other during the nights . . . By temperament a self-driving man in whatever he did----and thus pushing himself to the utmost in both occupations. It was his own fault. He did not have to drive himself like that. There was no family pressure on him. His wife Josephine was proud of his scholarly achievements primarily because he was himself. Though her mother was living with them and dependent on them, she was not one to nag about a good income. His father gave him constant sympathy and encouragement---and the interest of an intelligent man in his studies. The older Bandelier was one of those relatively rare individuals in the mundane midwest of the period, who knew that, though the pursuit of dollars was an inescapable necessity, the pursuit of knowledge was more significant and more satisfying. But the younger Bandelier was not one of those who could do things by halves. He was trying to be a definite success in two directions at once.

Along in the mid-1870's it was imperative that he relax some, take a prolonged vacation. He made it a busman's holiday. He spent it working as hard as ever----but in only one direction. He traveled in Mexico and Central America, digging into more original historical sources. . . And discovering that a lack of the scholarship in Spanish had led even historians of the calibre and reputation of William H. Prescott into serious errors.

Back in Highland, he was in double harness again----A curious split existence: By day struggling with the endless worrisome details of iron-casting and coal-mining; by night puzzling over and writing about Indian and Spanish antiquities. He was killing himself by more than inches now. But by the end of the decade he had completed and published, with Morgan's backing, four important monographs on the pre-Columbian Mexican Indians, three of them issued by the Peabody Museum at Harvard, the fourth by the American Association for the Advancement of Science.

That was his apprentice work in the field of Indian studies, the proving of capability. And finished just in time. In January of 1880, approaching his fortieth birthday, he suffered a serious breakdown, a severe case of nervous prostration.

One thing certain. No more business. No more trying to go in two directions at once. But how to earn a living in the one direction in which he wanted to keep going? Barely able to hold the pen, he wrote to Morgan pleading for help. A matter of "life and death", he called it----to get out of Highland and into some congenial work or become "a helpless idiot very soon". Any kind of a situation at all----"if possible as assistant librarian".

What? Bury that man with his superb linguistic abilities and the driving energy to do two men's completely dissimilar work for nearly twenty years in some obscure post in a stuffy library? Ridiculous!

It just so happened that the Archaeological Institute of America had been formed the year before and its major adviser was Lewis Henry Morgan. He was an old man now and soon to die. One of the last best things he did was to prepare for the Institute's First Annual Report a statement pointing out that "the most promising field" for archaeo-logical study in the United States was that of the Pueblo Indians of the southwest. And to urge in person and in letters that the man best fitted to undertake such work could be found in Highland, Illinois.

In a matter of months the Institute made one of the smartest moves of its own infant career. Out of its limited resources it agreed to give Adolphe Francis Alphonse Bandelier one hundred dollars a month to go forth and report on the living Indians and the ancient ruins of the American southwest.

The 21st of August, 1880. A slightly-built middle-aged man of medium height, dark-eyed, dark-haired, fair-skinned, boarded a train of the Missouri Pacific Railroad at St. Louis for the night trip across Mis-souri. Perhaps he slept some that night as the train rolled westward. Perhaps not. He had learned to get along with amazingly little sleep. Intense excitement simmered behind his seemingly mild and reserved exterior. In early morning, at Kansas City, he boarded a train of the still-new still-building Atchison Topeka and Santa Fe Railroad. All that day and into the evening he rode westward across Kansas and on to La Junta in the new state of Colorado. . . a courteous thoughtful man,

so quiet in manner that few of his fellow passengers even noticed him.
It was past midnight when the train left La Junta, southward bound towards Raton Pass and New Mexico Territory. Through the rest of
that night and on through the next day he watched in sleepless concentra-
tion the strange new land moving past outside the train and occasionally
he took a pen from a pocket to write in tiny script in a small notebook.
It was evening again when the train stopped briefly at a scrubby railsite
settlement that would be called Lamy in honor of a famous territorial
archbishop. He stepped down to step up into the stage that would take
him to Santa Fe. It was late night when he reached the old territorial
capital and registered at the Grand Central Hotel and went to bed.

His own record of that night of August 23rd, his first in Santa Fe, was
wonderfully neat and concise: "Slept till 9 A/M with bedbugs."

In the morning he went to the historic old Palace of the Governors on
the plaza to present his credentials to the territorial governor, General
Lew Wallace. The general was not there. The general was temporarily
afflicted with mining fever and was away on a jaunt of some forty
miles, probably to the Dolores gold diggings in the Placiere mountains
southwest of town.

Quietly he went about his own preparations. He was the first represen-
tative in the area of the new spirit of scientific research which was
taking over the whole field of ethnology and archaeology which had been
dominated so long by romantic notions and extravagant speculations.
Before leaving for New Mexico he had gone to Washington and consulted
with Major J. W. Powell, head of the Bureau of Ethnology of the Smith-
sonian, and Charles G. Rau, curator of the United States National
Museum. He had gone up to Cambridge and spent a week with Professor
Charles E. Norton of Harvard, president of his new collective employer,
the Archaeological Institute. Now, two thousand miles westward, he
was on his own, a one-man expedition, ready to begin the work for
which he was uniquely fitted. He planned to obtain his data from three
sources: study of old Spanish documents, investigation of ancient ruins,
personal experience with living Indians.

He called on people in town who might help him. He found, as he would
continue to find, that the Catholic Church, dominant through the southwest
since the Spanish Conquest, was and would be helpful and cooperative.
He had been raised a Protestant, but already he was leaning towards the
Catholic faith and eventually would be a convert. That attitude too was
a help with his work.

8

He checked into the official so-called archives and found them a confused mess. The American territorial governors, appointed from Washington, having little real interest in the territory, had paid scant attention to the Spanish records predating the American occupation. Some records had been sold to merchants for wrapping paper, others burned to conserve space. It would take a man like Adolphe Bandelier to make sense of what remained. He looked through them to see what would be available. He wandered out along the narrow unpaved streets of Santa Fe where three cultures met and mingled, Indian and Spanish-American and the recent Anglo.

Houses all adobe, some new . . . . Saw Pueblo Indians on the streets, fine fellows, clad in white with hair tressed behind and hanging down each side . . . . Meat (sheep and beef) hanging out on the portales, here . . . .

A fascinating old town. Nothing even remotely like it all the way eastward to the Atlantic. But there was work to be done. Five days after his arrival he was off on a field trip in a rented two-horse buggy to the ruins of the Pecos Pueblo near the rough tough little Spanish town of the same name in the foothills of the Sangre de Cristo mountains. With patient thoroughness he set about measuring the ruins and the entire site, collecting all remaining data and tales about it, exploring for other ruins in that rugged area. For a few days a photographer he had hired in Santa Fe was with him to take pictures of the ruins.

And at night, by the light of a candle in the little "boarding shanty" in which he was staying, he wrote to the old master back east in Rochester.

Everybody here is very much astonished at my discoveries; although they had the ruins before them for years and years. . . I am dirty, ragged and sunburnt, but of good cheer. My life's work has at last begun.

By the middle of September he was back in Santa Fe, working in the archives and hunting for old maps. A capable scholar. That could be taken for granted. But now he was demonstrating the speed with which he could work. On the 17th he dispatched a 95-page report on his "Visit to the Aboriginal Ruins in the Valley of the Rio Pecos", complete with pictures and maps, which would be published the next year in volume one of the Institute's American Series. Two days later——two days——he sent a 93-page paper, "Historical Introduction to Studies among the Sedentary Indians of New Mexico", which would soon be a classic in its field.

Withing a week he was off on another trip, to the pueblo of Santo Domingo on the Rio Grande, living there, sleeping "in the room of the priest in the old convent on a buffalo-hide". He hustled about, surveying and measuring the whole pueblo, drawing floor-plans of the buildings, jotting down innumerable notes on every aspect of the life of the people. Then he made what he himself later labeled "one of those errors which the novice in ethnology is liable to commit."

He was dealing here with living human beings, not dead ruins. The Santo Domingoans had welcomed him. They were feeding him. He was making a positive nuisance of himself and they were patiently accepting that in friendship. But he had brought with him an inevitable feeling of white superiority to what he regarded as stone-age laggards in historical evolution. He regarded them not so much as people as interesting objects for himself, a being of superior learning and knowledge, to study. Without being aware of it, he was haughty and somewhat autocratic in his attitude towards them. When he thought they were trying to trick or evade him in his investigations, he quarreled with the members of the tribal council. When the governor of the pueblo sought to reason with him, he let his temper get the best of him and kicked the governor out of his room.

Had he behaved that way with his own kind——with, say, the authorities in Santa Fe——he would have been chucked in jail and have been in serious trouble. Nothing of the sort happened at Santo Domingo.

> The next morning came a declaration of war in the shape of a refusal to give me anything more to eat.

Stubbornly he stayed on a few days, eating watermelons which he found in a nearby field. Scarcely a sustaining diet. Neither were his thoughts exactly palatable. He had made a mistake and he knew it. Not only as a research scientist offending the very people whose cooperation he needed in his work, but as a fellow human being. These stone-age laggards had taught him a lesson more valuable than anything he had learned in twenty years of hard study. Decency and dignity and forbearance had all been on their side in this affair. He left Santo Domingo a wiser and a humbler

10

man. He went up and across the river to the pueblo of Cochití and he went with an open heart and an open mind and he was received "with open arms" and given quarters in the house of one of the "principales" and accepted as a friend and a brother.

My relations with the Indians of this pueblo are very friendly. Sharing their food, their hardships, and their pleasures, simple as they are, a mutual attachment has formed itself, which grows into a sincere affection . . . . They begin to treat me as one of their own . . . . Of course, they have squabbles among themselves which often reveal to me new features of their organization; but on the whole they are the best people the sun shines upon.

Three months he stayed at Cochití, one of their own, living, as he put it, "in this 'Stone Age' of the past". He was learning the language, making drawings and paintings of the pueblo, of implements and ornaments, jotting down tales and legends and explanations of rituals and symbols freely told him. He was exploring the area and already had found twenty-four old ruins and diagrammed these and had been taken to see (and sketch) the hidden and legendary stone lions or pumas of the Cochití. Winter weather had set in and the temperature was often below zero and still he kept on, exploring the rugged mountainous area behind the pueblo, usually so busy that he rarely bothered to eat more than one meal a day.

It was during these months that he made his first discoveries, deep in the Pajarito plateau of the Jemez mountains, of the pueblo ruins and the remains of cliff dwellings and ceremonial caves in Frijoles Canyon, that great gash in the ancient rock——"the grandest sight I ever saw!"

As steadily, in free friendship, the Cochití took care of him, quarters always waiting, food provided, guides leading him where he wanted to go. "You have no idea," he wrote Morgan, "how much I am becoming attached to these Indians."

The southwest, that vast brooding land of distances and desert silences and great serene mountains where the past was so much a part of the present, in its own timeless way was making him one of its own.

On the last day of the year, 1880, back at Highland for the holidays with his wife and his father, he wrote in his journal: "Thus the most important year of my entire life draws to a close. . . . Have no reflexions to record. Future action is all that occupies my thoughts."

11

Future action! Plenty of it! During the next eleven years he was all through the southwest—not the southwest of the United States alone, but the southwest of North America. The boundary between Mexico and the United States set by the Gadsden Purchase and the Rio Grande meant nothing to the work he was doing. It was merely a contemporary political marking on a map. He was tracing the pre-history and the migrations of the Indians of the whole region above and below that contemporary boundary and filling in the history of the Spanish Conquest.

After the first field trip to Pecos Pueblo there were no more rented buggies and only rarely, for specific and easily accessible assignments, such luxuries as paid photographers. His one hundred dollars a month had to cover all expenses——supplies, living, travel, when possible the purchase of documents and maps and artifacts. All right. He could make a dollar go a long long way. He had his own two legs for transportation——and anyway buggies and even riding horses or mules would be useless in much of the rugged terrain he would be covering. He could sketch and paint with fair skill himself——and anyway few photographers would follow at any price the pace he would set into virtually unexplored areas.

Tens of thousands of miles he traveled, an amazing percentage of them afoot, all through the southwest, into almost every corner and crevice of it, across deserts and through mountain ranges, frequently alone, sometimes with a white friend, more often with an Indian companion or two. A quiet courteous tireless indomitable little man, walking, walking, walking through the great distances of a great land, armed only with a penknife (to sharpen his pencils) and a meter measuring stick and an invincible friendliness for his fellowmen of every race and creed, living off the land and the kindness of the native peoples, sleeping wherever night overtook him.

Not all Indians were friendly. Those were the years of the Apache wars. Unafraid, undeterred by any danger, he walked through them unharmed, his only precaution occasionally traveling by night and remaining quiet and hidden by day. Once he was taken by a raiding party—and sent on his way in peace. It was said that he was spared because he simulated insanity—and anyone so afflicted was regarded as sacred by the Indians. Perhaps so. More likely these Apaches understood that here, with little or no simulation involved, was a man touched with a kind of divine madness, a sacred intensity of purpose. They could understand such things. They let him go. They spread word about him.

12

Thereafter he was more or less free of the land they too roamed, free to wander unmolested by the roving raiding warriors who were keeping whole segments of the American and the Mexican armies busy with guerilla warfare.

Weather was a worse danger. He paid scant attention to it, went his way regardless of it. Once he and two companions were caught in a midwinter blizzard in the desertland of eastern New Mexico. They were separated by the blinding snow. The two companions perished—but he won through, riding some 90 miles through the drifts then tramping the last 35 miles through deep snow to safety. Again, alone in the winter bleakness of the Manzano mountains, he became seriously ill with small-pox. He came through that too, unaided, fighting off the sickness, tramping out to warmth and rest—and to continue soon on his lone way again. So persistent was he in his explorations that several times reports of his death were circulated. Ridiculous reports. The southwest was his life——not his death.

Had he been a "newspaper scientist", a self-pusher, a seeker after publicity, he might have achieved considerable prominence. He shunned it steadily. He was too busy for such nonsense. Titles annoyed him. When addressed as Professor, he would reply: "I profess nothing—if you would attach a handle to my name, let it be 'Mister'." As Doctor: "Don't 'doctor' me; I'm in perfectly good health, thank you!" The only approval other than that of personal friendship he sought was that of his fellow scientists—and he was not always respectful of them. When he thought they were wrong, he battled them vigorously in talk or in print. He was immovable in friendship once given—and an implacable enemy of what he considered error and fakery and false tradition. "I cannot conceive of anything in the world," said Charles F. Lummis, "which would have made him trim his sails as a historian or student for any advantage here or hereafter."

It was this same Lummis—writer, photographer, editor, wilderness wanderer, amateur archaeologist—who knew him well during some of the southwest years and after, who tramped hundreds of miles with him . . . . and constantly marveled at him.

One day. . .in the teeth of a particular New Mexico sand-storm that whipped pebbles the size of a bean straight to your face, a ruddy, bronzed, middle-aged man, dusty but unweary from his sixty-five mile tramp from Zuni, walked into my solitary camp at Los Alamitos. Within the afternoon I knew that here was the

13

most extraordinary mind I had met. . .I was at first suspicious of the "pigeon-hole memory" which could not only tell me some Queres word I was searching for, but add: "Policarpio explained that to me at Cochití, November 20, 1881." But I discovered that this classified memory was an integral part of this extraordinary genius.

Later, when Bandelier visited him at the pueblo of Isleta where he was staying, Lummis marveled again. When Bandelier arrived, "he knew just three words of Tigua. In ten days he could make himself understood by the hour with the Principales in their own unwritten language."

Lummis was an athlete, proud of his physical prowess; he had recently made a 3500-mile hike across the whole of the United States. Bandelier was "in no way an athlete—not even muscular". Yet not once in their long travels together did Lummis have to "slow down" for his companion. In fact, Lummis often had to use "laughing force" to make him stop at a good camping spot instead of "stumbling on through trackless night to an unknown 'Somewhere'." And why not? was Bandelier's view. There might be another undiscovered ruin just over the darkening horizon.

We had no endowment, no vehicles. Bandelier was once loaned a horse; and after riding it two miles, led it the rest of the thirty. So we went always by foot; my big camera and glass plates in the knapsack on my back, the heavy tripod under my arm; his aneroid, surveying instruments and satchel of the almost microscopic notes which he kept fully and precisely every night by the camp-fire (even when I had to crouch over him and the precious paper with my waterproof focusing cloth) somehow bestowed about him. Up and down pathless cliffs, through tangled cañons, fording icy streams and ankle-deep sands, we travailed; no blankets, overcoats, or other shelter; and the only commissary a few cakes of sweet chocolate, and a small bag of parched popcorn meal.

It was Lummis who made the most frequent trips with him to the Frijoles Canyon he had discovered and never tired visiting. They would start from Santa Fe, leading a burro with camera and equipment on it, and be gone for weeks at a time.

14

We were the first students that ever explored it . . . . What days those were! The weather was no friend of ours, nor of the camera's. We were wet and half-fed, and cold by night, even in the ancient tiny caves. But the unforgettable glory of it all!

Lummis, inveterate romantic and posturer, talked and wrote that way. For him the glory was in the adventure, in himself doing it. For Bandelier the glory was in the discoveries made, the archaeological evidence found, the knowledge gained.

For most of 1881 he was below the border, deep in old Mexico. He had expected to return almost immediately to New Mexico, but word came that he was to represent the Institute with a French research expedition in the Mexican province of Yucatan. He was on his way there when he bumped into the remnants of the expedition at Vera Cruz. The moist climate and tropical fevers of the Yucatan jungle had already proved too much for the members and the expedition was preparing to return to France. All right. He had been sent on a "ludicrous fool's errand". He would make the most of it. He was far south in Mexico; the Institute was still supplying one hundred dollars a month; he would be a one-man expedition again going on with the work begun in New Mexico. He went westward from Vera Cruz to Cholula, site of one of the most notorious massacres of the Conquest, and spent four months there studying its famous ancient pyramid that was larger than the largest in Egypt and the customs and beliefs of the native inhabitants. He moved on to Mitla and Tlacolula and Monte Alban, continuing his lone field work, exploring as always now for more ancient ruins. His "Report of an Archaeological Tour in Mexico, in 1881" would appear in volume two of the Institute's American Series.

Most of 1882 he was north of the border, making more sense of the archives at Santa Fe, visiting Cochití again for nearly a month, making field trips to most of the living pueblos and to ruins far down the Rio Grande valley. His report on these would be a major part of the first regular Bulletin issued by the Institute.

Just to trace his trampings through these years would tire the armchair traveler. Those of the winter of 1883-84 and on through the spring show a fair sampling.

15

He left Santa Fe in November and jogged down to the neighborhood of
El Paso where he spent two weeks among the Piros and Tiguas Indians.
Back to Santa Fe to work on the archives and follow some leads to old
San Juan, which had been the northern Spanish capital preceding the es-
tablishing of Santa Fe. Down-river again to Rincon and westward to
Fort Cummings and on to trace the Mimbres River to its source and
make explorations in that area. Over the continental divide to Sapille
and to the head-waters of the Gila River. On westward into Arizona
and to Tucson, then southwestward across the international border
into Mexico, into Sonora, following the Sonora River southward, stop-
ping at every village and vestige of human habitation on the way.
Apaches under Geronimo were operating in the region at the time.
He went right on. Up the Yaqui River, alone with his penknife and
pencils and measuring stick and little satchel of note-paper, past
places where the Apaches had struck, and eastward into the highest
reaches of the great Sierra Madre. Criss-crossings all through that
area and into the formidable Sierra de Teras, "until then untrodden
. . . as far as scientific research is concerned". Down the eastern
slopes of the mountains to Janas in Chichuahua, then southward some
to spend a month studying the massive ruins at Casas Grandes. Back
into the Sierra Madre to investigate the Arroyo del Nombre de Dios.
At last the long jaunt northward to Deming in New Mexico where civilized
travel by stagecoach and train was again available.

That was not straight tramping, following beelines from place to
place. It was wandering, purposeful wandering, with side explorations
everywhere and with pursuit of every hint of possible new discoveries
gleaned from natives at the few far lonely hamlets. One man, a complete scientific expedition in himself. During that six-month period
he had expended enough energy and accomplished enough research
to satisfy anyone else for a long resting time. But just a few days
after his return to Santa Fe he was off again on a swing to the northern
pueblos, starting with another visit to Pecos.

It was while far down in Mexico at Casas Grandes that he did a bit
of arithmetic in his journal, tallying the ruins he had discovered and
surveyed and measured.

Total of 84 in N. Mexico and 71 in Arizona, or 155. To this
should be added in Mexico 11, or 166 Ruins in 3 years. I
believe that this is a fair work. But do not let me become proud,
I may fall at any moment.

Late in 1884 his work was interrupted. Trouble at Highland. The family bank was in difficulties. He rejoined his wife and father there to see what could be done. He made a trip to the east coast (incidentally lecturing before the New York Historical Society) and even went briefly to Europe trying to obtain loans to save the bank. No luck. Early in 1885 the bank failed.

And now the Institute could not continue to pay that monthly pittance he had been stretching to such amazing results. All right. He would go on somehow on his own in the work he had started. He would continue his research and try "to make money if possible, by writing". He returned to New Mexico and to his field trips through the southwest. He continued sending reports to the Institute and even did scholarly treatises in various languages for publication abroad. These paid nothing. He did not expect them to. So he was writing newspaper articles, at space rates, and working on a novel——a novel of ancient Indian life based on his research at Cochití. His wife came from Highland to join him (his father would follow later) and they rented a house on old De Vargas Street in Santa Fe—— "to settle ourselves and take root permanently".

Hard times indeed in this 1885. "No resources, no money from no-where. Everything looks gloomy and dreary." He finished the novel—but he had written it in German because his thoughts flowed easily in that language. It would have to be put into English before he could hope to find a publisher and that would be a long slow task. But again the Catholic Church was a help. He wrote articles on the early Spanish explorers and the missionaries and on various Indian tribes for the Catholic Ency-clopedia. Archbishop Lamy at Santa Fe commissioned him to do "a history of the colonization and missions of Sonora, Chihuahua, New Mexico and Arizona" to be presented to Pope Leo XIII on the coming occasion of the pope's jubilee. He was at work on that and doing the kind of thorough job no other man of the period could have done. In due time the manuscript volume, 1400 pages of it with 400 watercolor sketches, would be presented to the pope for the Vatican library. Meanwhile the commission helped finance his continued field trips.

Hard times. But by the close of the year he had been named historio-grapher——to keep the records and write the history and search out documents——for the Hemenway Southwestern Archaeological Expedition. Not much more than a pittance again——but he was a man who could make a dollar go a long long way. This was his mainstay for the next three years. Some of the time he was in Mexico City, studying in the archives there, copying out documents pertaining to the southwest. Always he was working against clock and calendar, working fast, and writer's cramp became a serious and recurrent affliction. More of the time he was ranging far and wide through the whole vast region of the southwest, above and below the border, discovering more ruins, finding and preserving documents and manuscripts long thought lost, turning up others whose very existence had been unknown or forgotten.

His salary from the expedition grant ended with 1889. All right. There was more still to be done and he would do it, managing somehow. And so for several years more, a late-middle-aged indomitable little man doing a great work——rescuing the scattered dwindling documents of an important period of North American history and at the same time laying the foundation for all future ethnological and archaeological study of the southwest. Doing this on next to nothing in the way of financial support, only brief temporary assistances. He had translated his novel into English and at last, after many rebuffs, found a publisher, but the returns would be long delayed and uncertain. Mrs. Mary Hemenway of Boston, who had sponsored the southwestern expedition, commissioned him for some further work. The Institute contrived to contribute for a few months. A Santa Fe bibliophile financed a trip into Mexico for the purchase of the library of Father Fisher, the confessor of the ill-fated Emperor Maximilian. The New Mexican territorial legislature appropriated a small sum for more work with the local archives. With these and the proceeds of a few newspaper and magazine articles he managed to keep going. It was as hard work and as long hours as when he had been going in two directions at once——but there was no nervous collapse because all of it was in the one direction he wanted to go. He did it all and still was able to continue his field trips, those long swings tramping tramping tramping through the great distances of the land he had made so completely his own.

And to complete his two major writings of the whole period: the superb two-volume "Final Report of Investigations among the Indians of the Southwestern United States" and the valuable "Contributions to the History of the Southwestern Portion of the United States",

In May of 1892, approaching his fifty-second birthday, he wrote in his journal: "Thus the greatest undertaking of my life is done. . . Now begins a new period."

A new period, yes. But the same kind of work——and adequately re-cognized and financed at last. In July he sailed from San Francisco in charge of a well-staffed scientific expedition to do historical and archaeological research in South America. A new region, even a new continent——but not exactly a new field. This was still study of the past and the present of the Indians of the Americas and of the history of the Spanish Conquest.

The house in Santa Fe was closed down. His father departed for Switzerland, to the old home town of Berne, where he died in a brief while. Bandelier's wife went with him to South America. And there, only a few months after they had established headquarters in Peru, she too died. Something over a year later he married again, married Fanny Ritter, a member of the expedition, again of the appropriate Swiss ancestry, a native of Zurich, a linguist like himself, who became not only wife but secretary, assistant, partner in his work.

Ten years he remained there, in South America, the first two under the patronage of Henry Villard of New York, the remaining eight under that of the American Museum of Natural History. Still the same tireless explorer into the unknown of land and of native peoples. Peru and Bolivia were his country now, made his by explorations along the coast and into the highlands and on deep into the interior and by a sharing of the life of the native inhabitants. He became familiar with parts of the mighty Andes and with the jungles at the headwaters of the Amazon. Particularly intensive work was done on the islands of Titicaca and Koati in Lake Titicaca which lies between Peru and Bolivia and where archaeological remains and chances for ethnological study of the natives were exceptionally favorable.

In 1903 he returned to the United States to become directly associated with the American Museum and to prepare the results of those ten years for publication. He also accepted a lectureship at Columbia University in Spanish American literature with special reference to its ethnological and archaeological aspects. After a few years he left the Museum and continued writing on South American history for the Hispanic Society of America. He was suffering from cataracts now and for nearly three years was almost blind. But with his wife Fanny to serve as his eyes and hands he worked on, completing what many experts consider his finest single contribution, the full and detailed report on ''The Islands of Titicaca and Koati''.

Now, into his seventies, Adolphe Francis Alphonse Bandelier was thinking again of that "greatest undertaking" of his life, of the rugged roaring mountains and the vast enchanted deserts of the North American southwest, of the "fine fellows", the "best people the sun shines upon", who lived there and whose ancestors had for millenia and who had accepted him as one of their own. He had not forgotten any of it. He had not forgotten those satisfying years when he, a lone pioneer in a new field, a one-man scientific expedition in himself, had tramped his way into kinship with the land and its people. He had written papers at intervals through these last years from the notes he had taken there, among them the basic "Documentary History of the Rio Grande Pueblos" for the New Mexico Historical Review. He still regarded Santa Fe as his true home. That was where he had put down "permanent roots". He had not severed connections with the old capital. In absentia, by correspondence, he was a member of the staff of the Museum of New Mexico and of the School of American Archaeology whose headquarters were in the ancient Palace of the Governors on the plaza.

That greatest undertaking was not done——as he had foolishly written in his journal back in 1892. It would never be done. Always there would be more to do. He would return, as he had always intended, to the old capital in the heart of the Pueblo Indian country. But first there was more field work to be done. There were still ancient documents to be found, to be deciphered, to be made to yield their long-hidden secrets. In October of 1911 he accepted an appointment as a research associate of the Carnegie Institution in Washington for the specific purpose of completing his studies of the Spanish documentary history of the Pueblo Indians.

He went to Mexico City to work for months in the archives there. An old man, slowed down, but as skilled a linguist and as patiently thorough as ever. Then across the Atlantic to Spain itself to search through the archives of Madrid and Sevilla and Simancas. In March, 1914, in harness, at work on the greatest undertaking of his life, he died in Sevilla and was buried there.

His scientific writings remain on library shelves, still consulted by all who have followed him into the fields of knowledge in which he pioneered. Old-fashioned and out-of-date perhaps they are, and warped some by his loyalty to the theories of the master who gave him encouragement and launched him on his own career. But they remain, solid and sturdy, like a landmark for those who have followed and gone past him. His novel, The Delight Makers, is still in print and has been for more than seventy years. His collection of popular essays on the Spanish occupancy of America, The Gilded Man (El Dorado), has long been a collectors' item and has recently been reissued. Various collections of his letters have been published. In time, when the job of deciphering his microscopic script which is in many languages, skipping from one to another and back again according to whichever he happened to be thinking in at the moment, is finished, his journals too will be published. These are the kind of tribute he would have appreciated. But the best tribute of all is of another kind and is as enduring as the land itself——that great noble gash in the Pajarito plateau of the Jemez mountains, the canyon of El Rito de Los Frijoles, which a longtime friend named Woodrow Wilson designated by presidential proclamation to be preserved forever as Bandelier National Monument.

Strange things happen in the mystic magic of the deserts of the southwest. There are people who say that in the dimming dusk of evening when shadows slide across the sands and vision is bewitched, shadowy figures in the shape of men can be seen——ancient ancestors of the Pueblo Indians coming down from their cliff-dwellings to stalk deer and antelope; gaunt fanatical Spanish knights riding by with the fever of conquest glowing in their deep-sunk eyes; proud swift-footed Navajo warriors swooping to attack some quiet unsuspecting pueblo; old bearded prospectors stumbling in pursuit of ever-receding lost mines; outlaws, the Billy the Kids and the Marino Leybas, guns in hand, riding into legend; and lean fierce Apaches leading sweat-soaked frustrated cavalrymen on long bloody chases. Among them, through them, unawed by their weapons and warfare, at peace with all mankind, moves a slightly-built middle-aged man, unarmed and alone and afoot——tramping, tramping, tramping on the trail of knowledge and understanding of the long history of his fellowmen, with a small satchel full of microscopic notes in one hand and a measuring stick in the other.

AUTOBIOGRAPHICALLY SPEAKING

JACK SCHAEFER

I was born in Cleveland so damned many years ago that I can remember the day my father brought home the first family Ford with its brass front and oil lamps—and when I learned to drive it was still in a Model T. I came out of college just in time to meet the Great Depression head-on— and am still oldfashioned enough to think a national experience like that does more for a country than a Great Society. I was in newspaper work for sixteen years, all of it on the east coast, and rate that as some sort of apprenticeship in writing only because it was editorial work and on papers that still regarded editorial pages as more important than comics and sports and insisted on reasonable competence with knowledge and study and thought behind it. I was always a nut on American history and particularly Western history, so naturally my first book was a western. A little thing called SHANE. Since it did okay, in a sense I was lucky enough to start my freelance career some steps up the ladder. Didn't have to slug my way up the hard route. Maybe if I had, I'd be a better writer. Certainly not as lazy a one as time has proved me to be. Haven't averaged a book a year——and that is counting the slim little ones techni- cally as juveniles.

Five books and a start on a fair reputation as a writer about the west— and I had never been west of the Mississippi. Toledo, Ohio, was the furthest point reached and that when I was a youngster. Harry Sions (who was then at <u>Holiday</u>) thought that a sort of colossal joke and when he stopped laughing he suggested I go west at <u>Holiday's</u> expense. I did. I wrote him various articles (the Dakotas was first) and on one long jaunt my wife went along and as we returned to our place in Connecticut proved for the umpteenth time my wisdom in getting her to marry me by asking one simple question: "How soon can we move out there?" Two weeks later, with kids and cats and dogs and car and truck and in mid-winter, we were on our way.

I could never have written OLD RAMON or MONTE WALSH or even the latest little kid-book, STUBBY PRINGLE'S CHRISTMAS, without living here in the southwest. Yet nothing in all of the west, and I have covered most of it, some of it many times, has surprised me or seemed alien to me at all. It was in my bones long before I came here. I like what old Chuck Martin once wrote about me—that I was a Westerner who happened to be born in the east and had not come home yet. I've been home quite a while now. Years back, at eastern lit'ry parties (which I loathe and am glad to be f a r from) I used to argue there is no valid reason why a writer can not make an honest effort to create literature about the West just as surely as about the east or the south or any blamed place anywhere. In my lazy loafing land-of-mañana way I keep trying to prove the point.

December, 1964
La Gaceta
El Boletin del Corral de Santa Fe Westerners